Cara

Sheep Ahoy!

Poems and illustrations by Phil Sheppard

CONTENTS

Phil Sheppard is the author and illustrator of the
'Lollipopman' superhero books.
Visit www.lollipopman.co.uk

Published by

BAA CODE

www.baacode.co.uk

SHEEP AHOY!

I lost my sheep at sea
Don't ask me how
So I'm afloat
In a rowing boat
To get them all back now

Sheep Ahoy! Sheep Ahoy!
I see one out at sea
Zooming along
Singing a song
On a red jet ski

Sheep Ahoy! Sheep Ahoy!
It's surfing like a dude
Three setting sail
On a great big whale
That one's gonna be shark food!

Sheep Ahoy! Sheep Ahoy!
That one's lost its raft!
Off that island two
Are launching a canoe
There goes four on a hover craft!

Sheep Ahoy! Sheep Ahoy!
Five are sycronised swimming
Ten taking a trip
On a pirate ship
One stuck in a rubber ring!

So I found my sheep at sea
But I did it all in vain
Too many sheep!
I'm sinking deep!
...They're lost at sea again!

WHEN BISCUIT'S ATTACK!

When my dad raids the biscuit tin
He'll eat everything that's within
Now it's time the biscuits bit back
Make the Hobnobs fight
Make the Bourbons attack!

They'll nibble his knees
And torture his toes
They'll eat his ears
And gnaw on his nose

The Shortbread will be nasty
The Rich Tea mean
His bum will be bitten
By a Custard Cream

They'll run Party Rings around him
Then Fig Roll the old codger
He'll be P-P-Picked up by P-P-Penguins
And Jammed by a Dodger

The Jaffa Cake will go crazy
The Garibaldi barmy
How will Dad escape
This crazy biscuit army?

If Dad by now
Hasn't learnt his lesson
By this magic biscuit session
Then let the crazy Ginger NUT
Eat my dad from head to foot!

The Princess and the SHARK!

You know the story.

Princess.

Frog.

Kiss.

Prince!

Happy Ever After.

But you won't know about that princess's sister, Pearl!

Pearl wanted a prince, like her sister, Princess Jean.

But all she got
was warts...

and some nasty diarrhoea!

She kissed all the crabs...

She puckered up

...and smooched with a snail.

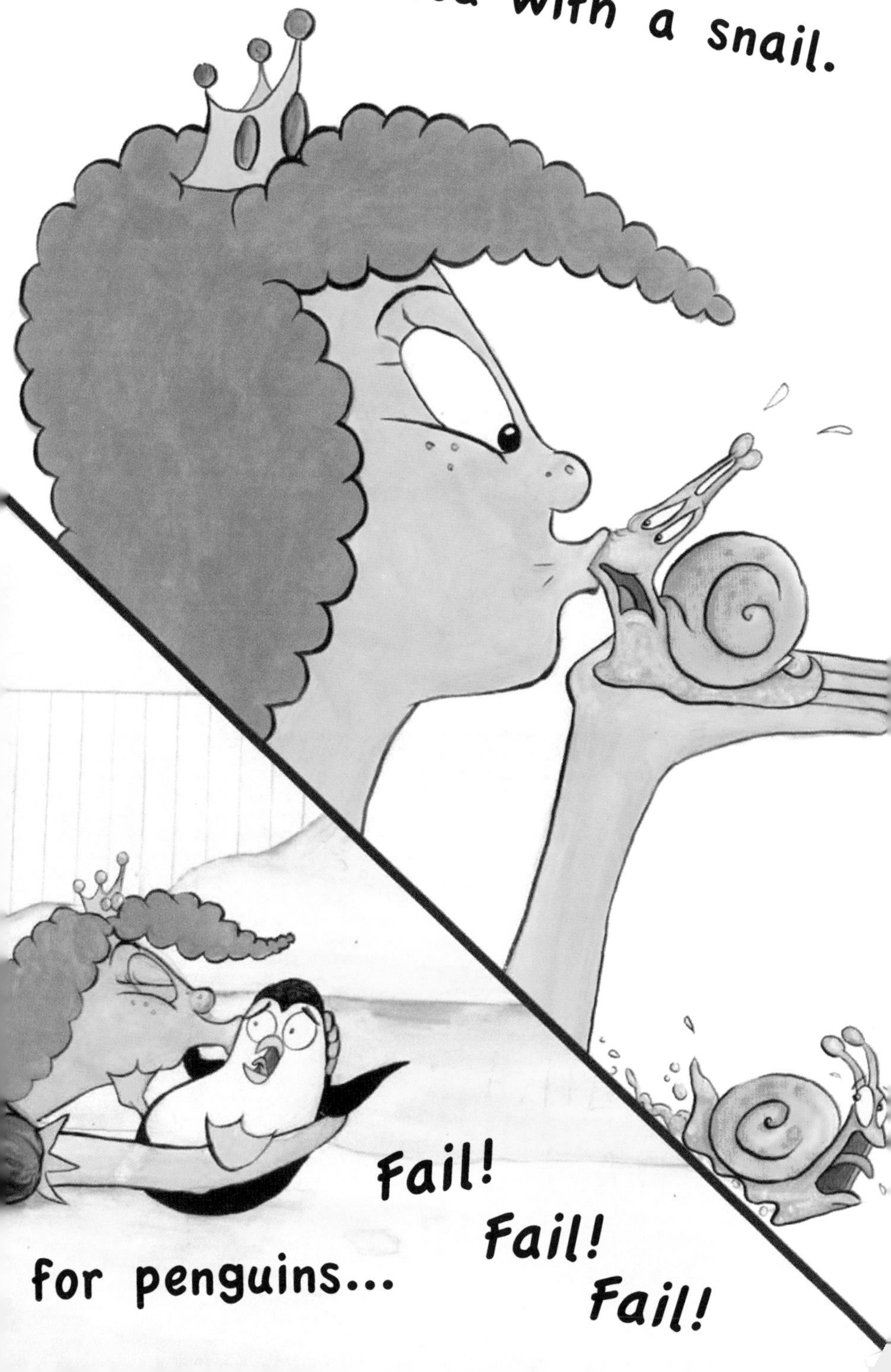

for penguins...

Fail!
Fail!
Fail!

went on a date with a duck.

She courted a crocodile...

but still she had no luck!

16

After kissing all the kingdom,

Which creature must I kiss

Pearl reached the sea:

to get a prince

for poor little

ME?

A horribly hungry shark
heard the
princess cry

and **BURST**
from the sea

with a *glint*
in his eye

20

When Princess Pearl returned,
she was **bursting** at the hips!

The shark licked his lips!

Mmm, you look ravishing honey!
What a cute little pup,
but I'm only gonna kiss ya
if you **sweeten** yourself up!

When she got back to the sea she was rounder than round!

The shark's stomach made a rrrrrumbling sound.

So Pearl
trundled off
and ate butter
by the tub,

piling it
on bread
and spuds

and other
stodgy grub!

The shark gave his
tummy a rub.

The shark opened wide,
happy with his tasty plan.

The princess puckered up, ready for her handsome man.

A

MAGIC
FLASH!

some

silver

stars!

Now where the princess

a whizz!

a FIZZ!

a SPARK!

had once stood was...

another,
BiGGER
shark!

The princess,
now a shark,
gave the smaller
shark a fright...

38

...and gobbled up
the mean
old thing

39

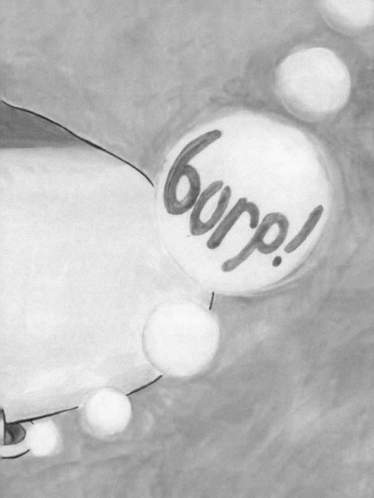

...with one colossal bite!

Backing a Winner

As they close the gate
The horses wait
All made of different things
At the horse of books
Nobody looks
Even though inside she sings
Most have no time for her
No one thinks that she's the best
But she knows imagination
Takes her further than the rest

AND AWAY THEY GO!

It's a horse made of pancakes
with chocolate syrup on the
top!
But there's syrup in the stirrups
and the jockey's fallen off!

Here comes the clothes horse!
Could this jumper have the
edge?
Oh no, she's come unravelled -
and run into the hedge!

It's the horse of pints of
Guinness - now there's a dark
horse!
But it's had too many
and it's staggered off the
course!

In comes a horse made of a
sofa,
Then a cantering coffee table!
The horse made of McDonalds
food
Is too fat to leave the stable!

And they're into the half mile

And the balloon horse has
popped,
the clock horse has stopped,
the glass horse has smashed,
the potato horse mashed,
the insect horse has flea-ed,
the Nintendo horse Wii-ed,
the tree horse falls,
the car horse stalls,
the egg horse is fried,
and the paint horse has... dyed!

*And they're into the quarter
mile -*

Could that purebread of pure
bread
pip them at the post?
Oh no! A dead heat with the
oven horse!
Now that purebread's pure
toast!

In the lead the horse of
televisions.
It seems this one could win
But it stops in its tracks,
it's been pulled back!
Haha! It's still plugged in!

Now one horse remains,
the pick of the pack
What a pace! What a thrill!
It's a paper-back!
Watch it go! Watch it go!
Galloping to glory!
It's Bookie the horse -
with Frankie DeStory!

42

ELEPHANTS

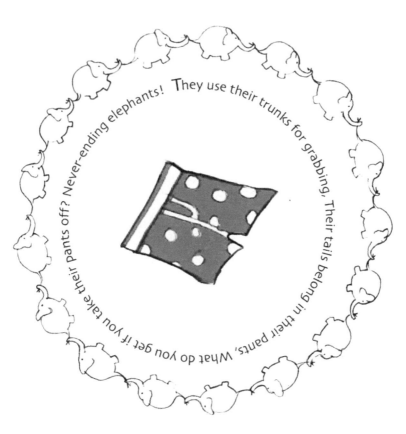

They use their trunks for grabbing. Their tails belong in their pants. What do you get if you take their pants off? Never-ending elephants!

The dog's snout is short... The dog's back is long! .... The top of the tail is fine... but underneath it there's a po 'ng.

The Dinosaur and the Dragon

Womp is a dinosaur

Womp likes being a dinosaur

Womp likes growling
and prowling
showing his teeth
being scaley
slamming his tail, he
likes snorting
and snarling
and scaring the bees
He likes being creepy
and sneaky
and taller than the trees

Most of all Womp likes running
Fast
Really, really fast
Indeed

Yes, it's cool to be a dinosaur
You're fast and scary and tall
Miles from the floor
Life's all gore, and claw, and gnaw
When you're a dinosaur

But, Womp wants more

Womp is a reptile
He's no Maths teacher
But one sum he does know:

Dinosaur + wings + fire
= a better creature!

A dragon.
Like a dinosaur
But better

Dragons can do everything dinosaurs can
But they can also fly
Through the clouds
And the sky
And breathe fire
They can burn
And fry
And barbeque
They're feared
And respected
And pretty cool too

No, Womp was not happy
With himself as he was
He wanted to be a dragon
With wings and a firey schnoz

One day, Womp was prowling
When he saw
Someone a bit like him
But it wasn't a dinosaur

It was a dragon
Just like he'd dreamed
With smokey nostrils and wings
Everything about her gleamed

"Hello" said Womp
"How are you today?"
The dragon turned, blew fire
Then flew right away

Womp gave chase
'cross the plain, through the sea
Till he caught up with the dragon
In the Womba Womba Tree

"I don't mean to be rude,
But I wanna be like you"
The dragon spun round,
Blew flames and flew

Through the clouds soared the dragon
Through the jungle ran Womp
Until they met again
In the Woop Wap Swamp

"Don't be angry" sighed Womp
"Wanna talk, that's all"
A turn. A scowl. A growl.
A great fire ball.

Womp gave chase
Swam the lake, jumped the fountain
Till he saw the great beast
Atop Wobble Mountain

"Please stay a while"
Called Womp through a gale
Till a great wave of flames
Singed poor Womp's tail

'cross the sea Dragon flew
In Womp dived
A little while longer
At the volcano they arrived

"Don't get mad"
Cried Womp to the beast
"Teach me to fly,
Or breathe fire at least!"

But dragon gave flight
Womp plunged back into the sea
And swam after the dragon
As North as can be

At last Womp came
To a colossal iceberg
Where dragon was seen
…but crying was heard

Dragon whimpered and wept
She looked ever so blue
She sniffed and sobbed
Womp didn't know what to do

Dragon quivered and shook
But Womp caught her eye
Dragon looked through her tears
"You're crying," Womp said, "Tell me why."

"I'm so lonely" she blubbed
"When someone says hello
I get so excited
At them fire I blow"

"Then I'm so embarrassed
That I just fly away
So I've never had a friend
To this very day"

Womp thought for a moment
Then offered his hand
"I'll be your friend
The best friend in the land"

So Womp learnt a lesson
From this beast from afar
That you should just be happy
With exactly who you are.

48

Poems

Some poems rhyme
Other poems don't
Write a poem that doesn't rhyme
I say I won't

I like poems that rhyme
I don't like the rest
Of all the lines in this poem
The *un*-rhyming one is the... least successful!

Never Babysit for a Giant

Never babysit for a giant
Cos when it starts to cry
It'll flood
The neighbourhood
And you'll never get it dry

Never babysit for a giant
Cos even when it's happy
It won't be long
Before that pong
Means changing a giant nappy

Smell no evil

SQUEGG

At dawn every morning
Farmer Fred Brown
Collects eggs from his hens
To sell in the town

As he opens the barn
And makes his way in
The hens stop to show
What they've been layin'

It's nine eggs from Nora
Six more from Maureen
Seven from Sybil
A dozen from Doreen

Four from Harriet
Wait! There's two more
Bertha's laid so many
She can't touch the floor

There's plenty from Primrose
Tons from Tabitha
Loads from Lilith
And ample from Agatha

Prudence looked proud
And Gladys had a grin
Both had their nests
Full up to the brim

Then there was Meg
At the end of the row
As sad as can be
Not one egg to show

"Never mind Meg,"
Said Fred to the chick
"One of these days
You'll come up with a trick!"

Fred picked up his basket
And climbed over the fence
Leaving poor Meg
To face the other hens

"Ha ha!" laughed Nora
"You really are dumb!
Not one single egg
Has come from your bum!"

Prim kicked poor Meg
Right up the rear
Meg fell head first
Holding back a tear

As the other hens laughed
At their barn mate's fate
Meg skulked out of the barn
And up to the gate

"If only they knew!"
She cried into her wings
"That I was able
Of much better things!"

The next day, at the farm
A car sped up the driveway
Fred's granddaughter Dawn
Was staying till Friday

All was going well
They were in a great mood
Till Dawn got hungry
And it was time for food

Fred and his wife
They cooked up a feast
The food looked delicious
To you and me at least

Yet at every yummy crumb
Dawn turned up her nose
"There's just no WAY
I'm eating one of THOSE!"

"I need three square meals
Every single day
This food is ROUND
I won't eat it! No way!"

She would not eat a thing
Unless it was square
The Browns tried everything
Till the cupboards were bare

Still Dawn ate nothing
And as the days passed
She got thinner and thinner
How would she last?

"Oh me!" cried Brown
"Oh dear dear dear!
If she doesn't eat a square meal soon
She's going to disappear!"

THEN! The door burst open
And they spun around to see
Little Meg Hen
As proud as can be

Meg turned round
To show her downy backside
Her beak closed tightly
Her eyes opened wide

She pushed! And she pushed!
The three stared in awe
Feathers flew all over
Then... it fell to the floor

Mr Brown gasped
And fell from his chair
For the egg Meg had laid
Was undeniably...

...square!

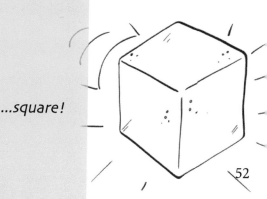

Brown had a brainwave
And leapt up from the floor
He dashed to the cupboard
Flung open the door

He pulled out a pan
Then a fork, then a knife
"Brace yourself honey
For the meal of your life!"

Brown made a fried egg
As square as can be
Dawn gobbled it up
Beaming with glee

Next came an omelette
With four equal sides
Dawn scoffed it fast
Then opened up wide

Up popped the toaster
Out toast was fired
For a square boiled egg
No egg cup required

Whether sunny-side-down
Or sunny-side-up
If it had four sunny sides
She just wouldn't stop

Poached, baked, scrambled
Finished off with egg custard
All cubic and scrumptious
"That really took the mustard!"

With a little burp
And an "Oops, beg pardon!"
Dawn got up
And went to play in the garden

53

The farmer and his wife
Looked down with pride
"I think it's time you
Moved your nest-egg *inside*!"

So from that day on
Whenever Dawn stayed
There'd be Meg in prize place
For the eggs that she'd laid

The other hens looked in
Through the rain and the snow
To see the hen they'd mocked
Sit with a warm, contented glow!

Waves look like this, You can swim in them all day; Sharks fins look like this... if you see one – swim awaaaaaaay!

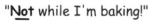
"**Not** while I'm baking!"

Turn
page
round

The Princess has to Pee!

The charming little princess
Sleeping sweetly in her bed
Dreaming of the seven seas
She rests her little head

"Ooo! Ooo! Ooo!
Eee! Eee! Eee!
Where's my potty?
I really need to pee!"

"Sorry," said the maid
"Can't help you with that
No potty here for you
Perhaps ask the cat!"

"Aah! Aah! Aah!
It's coming! Oh no!
Please give me my potty!
I'm BURSTING to go!"

"Meow," said the cat
"It's not me you need to pester."
"Squeak," went the mouse,
"Perhaps ask the jester!"

"Eep! Eep! Eep!
I can't take it any more!
If I don't go soon
I might pee on the floor!"

"Hee hee!" laughed the jester
"One too many teas?
You'd better ask the horses
Or learn to cross your knees!"

"Oof! Oof! Eee!
This feeling's getting worse
I feel like a balloon
That's just about to BURST!"

"Neigh," said the horses
"I'm afraid you're out of luck
No potty here for you
Perhaps ask the cook?"

"Shee! Shee! Sheesh!
I'm holding on tight!
Please fetch me my potty
Or pee right here I might!"

"Oh no," said the cook
"Your potty is not here.
Perhaps ask your sister
To help you out my dear..."

"Aaw! Aaw! Aaw!
No time to explain!
Fetch me my potty
Before I start to rain!"

"Ho ho little sis
Must be that special day
You should see the king
Come on now, this way!"

"Hello my Princess," said the King
"And Happy Birthday to you
You're a big girl now
So it's time to use the loo!"

I SPY

"I spy with my little eye
Something beginning with **T**"
"I'll get this one,"
Says father to son
"Just you wait and see."

"**T**ree!" says dad
"Nope!" says son
"**T**runk? **T**wigs? **T**imber?"
"Wrong! Wrong! Wrong!"

"That **T**rench? That **T**ent?
How about that **T**rail?
That **T**iny **T**abby cat?
That **T**abby cat's **T**ail?"

"Aha! A **T**own!
A **T**all **T**ower block
Tin roofs, **T**iles, **T**hatch?
The **T**own hall? The **T**own hall's **T**ick-**T**ock?"

"Or **T**raffic! **T**ransport?
Taxi? **T**ractor? **T**ruck?"
"We've passed the town dad,
you're out of luck!"

Dad looked at himself
"Oh my, oh my, oh my
How 'bout **T**eeth? **T**attoo? **T**oupée?
My **T**weed **T**rousers? My **T**artan **T**ie?"

"Here's some **T**rash:
Television! Bath **T**ub! **T**yres!
Or **T**elegraph pole?
Telephone wires?"

"Those **T**ermites! That **T**oad!
Thistles? **T**hicket? **T**horns?"
"Come on Dad!
You're not even warm!"

Then dad went quiet
He was just about to quit
Then he yelled, pointed down
"It's these **T**RACKS, isn't it!"

The son shook his head
"You've got it wrong a*gain*,"
He smiled, pointed forwards
"The answer is...

...that **T**rain!

8732330R0

Made in the USA
Charleston, SC
09 July 2011